Satchidananda Sutras

Jewels from the Teachings of

Sri Swami Satchidananda

"When hearing or reading sacred scripture, do not hear with the ear alone. It should go deep into the heart. Hear it with the entire mind.

"With such hearing, once is enough and you've got it. It's like dry wood. One match is enough."

– His Holiness Sri Swami Satchidananda

Publications by Sri Swami Satchidananda

Beyond Words

Enlightening Tales As Told by Sri Swami Satchidananda

The Golden Present

Guru and Disciple

The Healthy Vegetarian

Integral Yoga Hatha

Kailash Journal

The Living Gita

To Know Your Self

Yoga Sutras of Patanjali

Publications about Sri Sw. Satchidananda

Sri Swami Satchidananda: Apostle of Peace

Sri Swami Satchidananda: Portrait of A Modern Sage

The Master's Touch

Satchidananda Sutras

Jewels from the Teachings of Sri Swami Satchidananda

Pocket Edition

Compiled by Lakshmi and Paraman Barsel

Epilogue by Rev. Prem Anjali, Ph.D.

Integral Yoga® Publications, Yogaville, Virginia, USA

www.yogaville.ORG

Pocket Edition   ISBN 0-932040-53-5

© Copyright 2002 by Satchidananda Ashram-
Yogaville.

All rights reserved, Integral Yoga ® Publications

Satchidananda Ashram-Yogaville, Buckingham,
Virginia 23921, USA

www.yogaville.ORG

Table of Contents

Guru Guru Japna

Aur sab Swapna

Meaning: Do japa Guru Guru
All the rest is dream.

Guru Guru Japna, Aur Sab Swapna.
Meaning: Do Japa 'Guru Guru,' All the Rest is Dream.

Dedication

This booklet is dedicated to our Beloved and Revered Sri Gurudev, His Holiness Sri Swami Satchidanandaji Maharaj, who is a pure reflection of the Divine Self, an infinite ocean of compassion, the embodiment of perfection in action, from whose heart the Eternal *Dharma* flows, bringing comfort, guidance, and inspiration to sincere seekers everywhere.

On 19 August 2002, His Holiness Sri Swami Satchidananda (Sri Gurudev) attained *Mahasamadhi* (a God-realized soul's conscious final exit from the body) in his native Tamil Nadu, South India. The *Mahasamadhi* rituals and interment ceremony took place on 22 August 2002 at Satchidananda Ashram-Yogaville. Though Sri Gurudev changed His form, He promised us that we remain united with His enduring Spirit. We are eternally grateful to Him.

Acknowledgements

This booklet was published in conjunction with the "Victory to the Light" program held at Satchidananda Ashram-Yogaville, Virginia, on 18–20 October 2002. This program provided an opportunity for the Integral Yoga family to come together to offer our love and respect for our Beloved Sri Gurudev. We are forever grateful that Sri Gurudev's yogic example and teachings continue to provide us with a spiritual foundation, giving us the capacity to receive His Divine Guidance and experience His Eternal Presence always.

We are grateful to Lakshmi and Paraman Barsel for this beautiful compilation of some of the most profound of Sri Gurudev's utterances. For a number of years, Lakshmi and Paraman have offered workshops and evening programs in Yogaville based upon the *Satchidananda Sutras*. It is wonderful to have these Sutras now in booklet form, so that everyone who wishes may drink deeply from the wellspring of Sri Gurudev's Enlightenment.

Special thanks to Rev. Prem Anjali, Ph.D., for the epilogue that follows the Sutras. We also wish to thank Prakash Shakti Capen for offering her editing skills,

Shiva Alain Hervé for designing the booklet, and Sr. Karuna for production assistance.

Introduction

Our Beloved and Revered Sri Gurudev Swami Satchidananda Maharaj is that rarest of treasures in the universe, an enlightened Master whose every word is scripture, whose every utterance serves to bring us closer to experiencing and abiding in His own infinite Consciousness. With such a supreme Satguru, finding priceless jewels amongst His words is as easy as breathing. The only difficult task is choosing which gems to include in this brief offering. His bounty is truly endless!

These Sutras – potent essential teachings – are culled directly from His spoken satsangs and occasionally augmented from His writings. They are presented in His own words, with no need of commentary. Sri Gurudev's words have always possessed the exquisite compactness of the greatest Divine poetry. Like many of His favorite scriptures – the *Yoga Sutras* of Patanjali, the *Bhagavad Gita,* the *Thirukkural,* and Saint Avayar's teachings – Sri Gurudev's extemporaneous words pack vast truths, limitless light, unconditional love and endless enlightenment into the most compact of forms. Even one of these *Satchidananda Sutras* is enough to transform one's entire life, to remove the darkness of ignorance and to reveal the Light of Wisdom.

May God bless all who seek nourishment herein with that liberating Grace that is the eternal Guru whose Spirit is alive everywhere and especially in the hearts of His devotees.

Lakshmi and Paraman Barsel

Satchidananda Ashram-Yogaville, Virginia

Happiness and Fun

You are happiness personified.

The primordial sin is forgetting that we are happy already by nature.

When we forget we are happy already, we want someone or something to bring us happiness, and then we are bound.

The purpose of the whole world is to teach us that happiness from the outside is mixed with unhappiness.

Every scripture, every great thinker, every sage, every saint has told us, "Please do not look for everlasting joy from anything on the outside."

Nothing can make you happy. If something makes you happy, it is a borrowed happiness.

When you go after something hoping that it will make you happy by getting it, you have already traded away your peace.

Nothing will make you always happy. Things are given to you to be used for public service.

The minute you free yourself from depending on outside people and things for your happiness, you feel the joy.

Happiness and unhappiness are in the mind.

If you want to be happy, renounce the "I, me, mine."

If you are free from any want, you are the happiest person.

If you are contented in life, happy by yourself, you don't have to cause injury to anyone.

Health is being perfectly comfortable and happy in all situations.

Yoga began with the first person wanting to be healthy and happy all the time.

Everything is fun if you know the secret.

To have fun, be a good witness.

Life is fun. Life is dualities. Someone should praise you. Someone should blame you. Otherwise it is not fun.

Recognize the non-changing Self and the ever-changing. Only then can you have fun.

Life itself should be a game.

Anything you do, you should do with all joy. Play. There is nothing serious. Play your part.

Peace

If you don't have peace, you have nothing.

The moment you feel your peace slipping away, immediately say: "No, I care more for my peace than anything else. I just want peace and peace alone. I'm worshipping my peace."

When anything comes to you, first ask yourself, "Will I be maintaining my peace by getting this, or will my peace be disturbed?"

Peace is God. But even if God comes to disturb your peace, send Him away.

The less you think about yourself the more peaceful you are.

Become a peaceful person. At least then you will not be a nuisance to anyone. You become a nuisance by wanting something (desires) or not wanting something (aversion) for yourself.

To be peaceful, you should have no "wants" and no "don't wants."

Even a little expectation will make you lose your peace.

If you lose your peace, you are unfit to serve yourself or to serve others.

Find peace first and then you can go out and help the world.

If you are easeful and peaceful, you will be useful.

Karma Yoga – The Yoga of Action

Doing things for others without expecting anything back is a form of worship. That's Karma Yoga.

The dedicated ever enjoy Supreme Peace. Therefore, live only to serve.

Service means one-way traffic – giving, giving, giving. It is not business.

A joyful and happy life is possible only when you dedicate your life for the service of the entire creation.

If you realize that whatever you do to others – including animals, people, plants, minerals, elements – you are doing to God, then you will know that your main purpose in life is to serve God's creations.

When you know that your main purpose in life is to serve God's creation, then you successfully brush aside the egoistic mind – the "I, me, mine."

Once you are free of selfish desire, you work for the joy of it and all your actions are as a *leela* (play).

Real freedom is enjoying whatever you do.

If you love what you are doing, you never become exhausted.

If you keep your eye on your work, you do not know sleep, or hunger, or hear what others are talking about.

A person who is not interested in the fruits of his or her actions should do a better job because the idea "I want to get" creates an anxiety that pollutes the mind.

Know that we are all here to serve others just as all of Nature is here to serve others.

You'll never face any disappointment or depression if you make your entire life an offering.

Don't live to eat, eat to live, and live to serve.

Eating, talking, walking, everything should be done to serve others. If this is your motto then you are living God's Life.

No one needs your service. With Karma Yoga, you have the opportunity to train body and mind. We are not doing something for anyone else. We are doing it for ourselves.

When you offer yourself for service, your motivation is always tested.

You do not need to learn to serve. You need to know that you are already serving.

Strictly speaking, we are all serving: God makes you do things; God makes you God's instrument and uses your body, mind, senses, everything. The problem is that unnecessarily you take it on your shoulders, "I did."

Unfortunately we say, "I did it. I gained it. I lost it." You never did anything. It's all being done by God.

When you successfully brush aside the egoistic mind, you will be able to perform miracles because the God in you does everything for you.

When you know that someone or some force is behind everything, you know that nothing is impossible.

An action without any selfish expectation whatsoever is a right action. Such an act will never disturb your mind or body.

If you do things with the proper attitude, you know the loss or gain is not yours, and it will not disturb the mind.

Man me Ram. Hath me kam. Mind on God, hand on work.

Whatever you do to others including animals, people, plants, minerals, elements, you are doing to God.

Everything has life; everything is the image of God, even a stone, even a weed. But everything should be in the right place. If you see a weed, talk to it, "Sorry you are growing in the wrong place. I have to pull you out. God bless you." And pull it out.

God created you for a purpose and only you can do the job.

The cosmic intelligence takes care of everything. It puts you in certain places; and when you finish there, puts you somewhere else.

A perfect (yogic) act should bring some benefit to someone and no harm to anyone.

Bhakti Yoga — The Yoga of Devotion

God can manifest in any form, with any name. You can worship God anywhere.

You can just pick up anything and if you call it "God" with all your heart, it becomes God because God is everything.

God is in you, working through your body and mind every minute. You are never alone. God is nearer to you than your own heart.

Only the formless can be made into any form. Only the nameless can be given names. Only the unconditioned can be brought into any condition. That's why we say God's love is unconditional.

All names are God's name; all forms are God's form.

It's all Your Name. It's all Your Form. It's all Your Deed. It's all for good.

Choose any name, form, etc. The important thing is sincere faith, a child-like heart.

God is not interested in your words of learned length and thundering sounds. He wants your heart.

The form of worship or ritual is not important. God wants your heart.

If you sincerely cry for God, God will come running and give you everything.

Whatever you do should be done as a form of worship.

Whatever you do becomes worship if you do it with the right feeling.

When you have *viveka* (discrimination), true devotion arises.

True devotion to God is doing something with the feeling that you are ultimately using and approaching the same consciousness which is taking expression in different forms.

The real meaning of worship is seeing God in everything.

Who wants God? The miserable man.

When will you want God? When you are tired of everything else.

If you are fully tired of everything else — 100%, — you will go for God and never turn back.

When you are tired of everything, you will find permanent *vairagya* or non-attachment and then you will want only God, God, God.

That's why nature makes everything fail so we can turn around to God.

Experiencing God is easy only for the person who really gets sick of the other side, of trying to experience everything else.

Faith

The backbone of every ritual is sincere faith.

Faith can work wonders.

If you have complete faith in God, you can drink poison and it will become nectar.

To develop faith, analyze your own life, you will see an unseen hand taking care of you every minute, every second.

We live on faith. Even your life depends on faith.

Have faith but don't take everything literally. Your faith alone will carry you a long way until you understand everything.

Each of us has our own faith but we all have the same goal – to experience God.

Put your faith on something useful, something helpful, but even if you put your faith on something that is not useful, it is useful because you will learn from your mistakes.

If you have total faith in the Supreme Power, you won't be afraid of anything.

Faith and fear don't go together.

The fearless person never dies. The fearful person dies every minute.

If you really trust God, you must trust in both the profit and the loss.

Know that God is always taking care of you. Even before you are born, God is preparing the food for you in your mother.

If you know that God is taking care of you, you have nothing to worry about.

Prayer

The best prayer is: God, let me remember You always. Your hand is everywhere. You do everything to me. Without You, even the atom could not move.

If you want to have a prayer, pray to God to help you to always remember this truth: that you are His child and He is taking care of you every minute.

The highest form of prayer is to just enjoy praying and praising God without asking for anything.

A true devotee doesn't even ask God for anything. He knows that God will give him everything he needs even without asking.

God will not give you anything that is not good for you, even if you ask for it.

Don't allow your pride to get between you and God's help.

It's only when you say, "I can't do it anymore, please help me," that the help comes.

The real prayer comes after you finish speaking.

It's not the head that prays; it's the heart.

Deep prayer always comes from the heart.

In deep prayer you forget everything. You lose yourself. You become God and you can do all that God does.

Prayer from a pure heart can work wonders.

Prayer should be totally heartfelt, then it is a meditation combined with prayer.

By your concentrated, sincere prayer, you are tuning your mental radio to receive God's omnipresent power.

When you tune your mind to the proper wavelength, you will receive God's Grace and experience Cosmic Consciousness.

Love

Love can melt stones.

Love can change anything and anybody.

To love properly is to put no conditions at all.

Unconditional love is when you love without expecting anything in return.

Unconditional love is when you love because you like to love.

Totally unconditional love is a pure love.

Unconditional love can transform everybody.

Nothing is impossible if you have unconditional Love.

Let your love be universal love. Love everyone and everything equally.

Universal love is only possible when you see everything as an expression of your own Self.

Let us make a resolution: I will not bring any harm to anyone by using my love in an improper way; nor will I look for anything in return. I am content just to love.

Let our love bring good, and good alone, to everyone.

Selflessness

Selflessness is the key to spiritual life.

Completely free yourself from selfishness.

A selfish person is always agitated.

Even with a little selfishness, you are bound.

Every problem comes because there is a little bit of selfishness in it. Whatever you do, you want something in return.

Anything you do with a selfish motive will go wrong.

If you realize that all suffering comes from selfishness, you won't want to be selfish anymore.

Renounce the selfishness and you will be in bliss.

Keep the mind clean of selfishness, that is true Yoga, that is the purpose of the Yoga practices, of meditation.

If you are selfless, praise or blame – it doesn't matter. Pleasure or pain, it doesn't matter.

All of Nature is giving, self-sacrificing. The candle sacrifices itself to give light. The incense stick sacrifices itself to give fragrance.

Always live for others, do for others, think of others. Automatically your needs will be fulfilled.

The ego is the root cause of all the troubles.

Your ego binds you. A completely selfless life frees you so you can experience your own natural state of peace and joy.

If you could set aside the "I, me, mine" and use the ego for the service of others, whatever you do is okay.

When the ego is gone, all the divine qualities are automatically there in you.

Make your desires selfless desires; that means you desire for the sake of others.

Selfless desires will not bother or weaken the mind.

Non-attachment

Attachments are what bind us. The more attachments we have, the greater the bondage; no attachments, no bondage.

Don't think that marriage is only between a man and woman. You are married to everything you are attached to.

Not only a boy and a girl get married. You are married to everything you possess. You are married to your mind, your senses, your wealth.

Whatever you are attached to, you will get divorced from.

It is attachment that causes fear.

The biggest attachment is "I, me, mine." That is the worst and biggest covering of the heart.

To see how close you are to God, make a list of everything you call "mine." The longer the list, the further you are from God.

When you have a lot of "mines" around you, you are living in a mine field.

A "mine" will explode on you. It was never yours. You didn't bring anything and you are not taking anything with you. In-between it was given to you, not to own, but for your use.

You didn't come with anything. You won't go with anything. Come with nothing. Go with nothing. Use what is given to you for God's work.

If you lead that kind of detached life, God will know and give you more to use for public service.

Real strength, inner strength, comes from being clean at heart, from renouncing your mental attachments, your I, me and mine.

Lead a simple life. First reduce your "greeds." Then reduce your "needs."

"*Kita dayin vetana mara*. If you don't get it, immediately forget it."

Make no appointments. Get no disappointments.

By having no expectations, you will remove the veil over the inner Light.

If you don't want, all will want you.

"*Atra du patra nil, utra du veedu*. Drop your wants and you are home (enlightened)."

No more desires, no more bodies.

Sannyas – Renunciation

Not by doing, not by progeny, not by wealth, not by wisdom, not by education, not by scholarship, but just by renouncing everything, you experience the truth.

Whoever you are, wherever you are, you need to give up.

Give up everything then you get everything.

Let your desires drop away, that is the best renunciation.

Renunciation does not mean that you negate everything, that you are indifferent and run away. No, it is just being neutral.

To renounce, simply love everyone and everything without attachment.

Real renunciation means freedom from selfishness.

Renounce your selfishness and live for others.

Who is a *sannyasi* (renunciate)? One who has renounced selfishness.

Who is my most cherished devotee? The one who possesses nothing.

You are all *sannyasis* (renunciates). You don't have to change the name or wear a different dress. There is *sannyas* (renunciation) in you all.

If you feel: "Everything is given to me for God's use; nothing belongs to me," you are a *sannyasi*.

Perform everything as your duty. Then you are a *sannyasi* (a renunciate), wherever you are.

In *sannyas* you renounce your individual family, not by negating them, but by expanding your family to include all as your brothers and sisters under one God.

Don't expect that the minute you decide to renounce, everybody will immediately take care of you. You have to prove your sincerity first.

Be in the world but not of the world.

You should be like a boat sailing on top of the world and carrying others. If you let the world into the boat, it cannot even hold itself up.

Divine Will

Nothing happens without God's will.

Without God, not even an atom can move.

Your so-called free will is part of that Cosmic Will. It's like the ocean and the wave.

Use free will to freely align yourself with the Divine Will.

If you trust in the Higher Will, all the obstacles will just disappear.

Know that every minute that great Presence is in you, functioning through you, and you are nothing but an instrument. The highest realization is that.

The minute you realize that God is doing everything through you – that it's not your doing, you don't need to worry about anything.

In a way, all problems are God's problems. We are all tools in the hands of God.

When are you really living? When you realize you are not the doer.

From a higher perception, everything has been ordained already. It was all decided long before.

Mind

"*Mana eva maneshyam*. As the mind so the man."

You are a thinking being. You make yourself as you think. Because your mind makes you, you are the product of your own thinking.

One disturbed mind can affect the entire world.

The mind causes all the problems of the world and at the same time it brings you all the benefits.

If you might hurt someone with your speech, you should think before you think, or at least think before you talk.

Speak sparingly. A word is a bird. Once let out, you can't whistle it back.

To not cause pain, you must have tremendous capacity and control of your thoughts.

Be aware of what your mind is doing by keeping a watchful eye on your own thoughts and actions.

Choose your own way to keep the mind steady but keep the goal in mind.

The greatest victory ever won was not in war but victory over the mind.

Self-mastery over the mind is the greatest victory. That is the reason you do all of the Yoga practices.

With mastery over the mind, you can move mountains. Christ called it faith. He said, "With faith the size of a mustard seed, you can move mountains."

Once you gain victory over the mind, the mind submits to you.

Before you proceed, you should know what your goal is. The goal behind everything – even mastery of the mind – is just to be happy.

When you have complete control over your mind, you have controlled everything.

Get rid of all bad thoughts by pure thought. Get rid of pure thoughts by one thought.

If you think of anything, think of only one thing at a time.

The mind is a bundle of thoughts. Like a bundle of things, when you get rid of all the thoughts, there is no more bundle.

When the mind is totally free of thoughts, there is no more mind.

Having a steady mind, a balanced mind is what you call purity of heart.

"Blessed are the pure in heart, they shall see God." How is the heart made pure? By making it free from thoughts.

Purity means neutrality.

The peaceful mind is like a clean mirror. It becomes a well-tuned receiver of the transmissions of the universe.

When it is clean and clear, the mind doesn't color the appearance of the pure Self. It becomes a pure reflector of the Self to see its own true nature. That is the essence of spirituality.

With a peaceful mind all knowledge, all wisdom comes to you.

To practice Yoga, you need a one-pointed mind. Once you get that, then prosperity, bliss and peace of mind are yours.

Emotions

If you have a conflict within yourself, ask what the reason is. Then you will see it is your own expectation, your own wanting, your own attitude.

Minds are all different. Accept it. The problem comes when you want them to think the way you want.

Acceptance is most important in resolving conflicts between individuals and groups.

No one can provoke you. No one can make you happy or unhappy. You are the one in control.

No one has the capacity to make you angry or happy. You are the cause of your own anger or happiness.

You should never actually become angry. Just keep anger in you pocket. If you need it to clear up an injustice, use it. Then put it away again immediately.

Spiritual Practice

Take it easy but not lazy.

Anyone can go and close their eyes and meditate. Even rocks do that. Trees do that. Adapt, adjust, accommodate, bear insult, bear injury is the highest *sadhana* (spiritual practice).

Bear insult, bear injury is the highest Yoga.

Accept insult and injury and return a good job.

Don't harbor any insult or injury in your heart. If you harbor, you become a junkyard and you will ruin your mind and ruin your health.

Anytime you find someone accusing you, look within and ask, "What did I do to make this person do that?"

When you point your finger at someone in blame, three fingers point at you, so correct yourself.

For one week follow all the teachings of Yoga and you will not want to do anything else.

Spiritual practices should be done because you want to do them, not because someone else wants you to do them.

You do your spiritual practices for yourself and no one else.

Satsanga (company of the wise) is all of your yogic practices: studying scriptures, Hatha Yoga, meditation, Karma Yoga.

"*Satsangatwe Nisangatwam*
Nisangatwe Nirmohatwam
Nirmohatwe Nishchalatwam
Nishchalatwe Jivanmukti
"When you are in good company,
   you are not in bad company.
When you are not in bad company,
   you are free from delusion.
When you are free from delusion,
   you are steady.
When you are steady,
   you are a living, liberated being."

You need to do your spiritual practices for a long time without a break and with total faith, total zeal.

It's not easy. If you get it easily, you will lose it easily. Anything hard-earned you will know the value of it.

Perseverance brings perfection.

Don't keep changing – digging lots of shallow wells. Stick to one and get it done.

Pick one thing and stick to it.

Ultimately you must liberate yourself from your practices too, but don't be in a hurry.

There is a natural maturity for everything. If you are forcing somebody to do something before the maturity comes, it creates more problems.

The head, heart, and the hand should develop simultaneously.

Spiritual practices should never be followed blindly. Go deep. Get some experience to be convinced.

Seek the Kingdom of Heaven first and everything else will be added unto you.

Everything that belongs to God belongs to you so seek
That first. This is the aim behind spiritual *sadhana*
(spiritual practice).

Everything is Yoga. Touch everything with the magic
wand of Yoga and you will see Yoga everywhere.

Meditation

Meditation is the key to everything.

Mere knowing and doing are not enough. Put your entire mind on it: meditate on it.

Meditation is total focus of the mind, one-pointedness.

Everything can be done as a meditation.

Don't think that only when you close your eyes, you are meditating. Anything that you do with total attention is meditation.

Do all that you do as a meditation.

When you eat, meditate on eating.

If you want to get out of the problem of depression, practice meditation. Strengthen your mind.

By meditation, you make your mind strong and powerful. You need a strong and powerful mind to accomplish anything in life.

If you meditate regularly, you will have no complaints in life.

Preparation for meditation is more important than the meditation itself.

When you stop making outside noise, you hear God's voice within.

You can do hours and hours of meditation or mantra repetition, but in those 1000s of times, if just once your real heart is into it, that's enough.

Mantra – Sacred Sound Formula

The best spiritual practice in this age is mantra repetition.

Japa Yoga (mantra repetition) is the best practice – what a person cannot do, a person's mantra can do.

That little mantra brings out your own sound vibration to the surface.

A mantra has tremendous power but you must bring it out. You must care for it in the beginning, very much like caring for a young plant.

Your mantra is like a pillar. Hold onto it and go round and round. If you let go, you will spin away.

Sometimes you don't want to do selfish things, but your mind makes you do it. You can gain mastery over your mind by practicing mantra repetition.

Wear the mantra as your armor. There's no greater power than that.

If you take mantra initiation from a Guru, it is like taking a little of the Guru and implanting it in you. It is like making yogurt from milk.

Anything atomized has more power. God's name is atomized power.

If the mantra, or God's name is solidified, it becomes God with form. If God with a form becomes liquefied, it is mantra, a sacred sound vibration. The sound is more powerful.

Let my tongue repeat the mantra even if my mind does not.

Prana (vital force) is more powerful than the physical level. Mantra is beyond *prana*.

If your mantra has a meaning, repeat it with the meaning in mind.

A mantra without a meaning will have a seed word *(bija)* that has a sound vibration. By repeating it, you will awaken the sound vibration which is dormant in the lower area of the body called the *kundalini*.

God's very first manifestation is the sound.

Even if you forget Hatha Yoga, breathe. If you forget to breathe, at least remember the mantra.

Willpower

You can do whatever you want, you can achieve whatever you want if your will is strong enough.

Practice Yoga and develop that willpower not to succumb to the whims and fancies of the lower mind.

Gradually develop your willpower by doing small things, taking little steps.

If you want to build your willpower, start with a *sankalpa,* a strong decision or vow. This will take you halfway to achieving your goal.

If you stick to your vow, you control your mind.

Beauty and Art

Everything is Divine Art. See the art from the heart. Make your *sadhana* (spiritual practice) seeing the art in everything.

People who use the head do not see the inner beauty. For that you need the heart.

Inner beauty is the real beauty.

Don't worry about cosmetic beauty. You will get the cosmic beauty.

A baby needs no make-up; it glows with God's light. You lose that glow because you begin to worry and get too many attachments.

The ability to see beauty and to be beautiful depends on a clean, pure, balanced heart.

Beauty is in the eye of the beholder. If your eyes are ugly, you will see ugly.

Strictly speaking, the eyes do not see, the mind sees. Make your mind beautiful and you will see beauty.

If your heart is beautiful, your face will be beautiful, your life will be beautiful, everything will be beautiful.

When you see beauty in everything, you will progress spiritually.

If you have a clear mind that is the beauty in you.

With a good, clean heart, you will see everything as beautiful. That is the Divine Vision.

Marriage – Relationships

Real marriage is when two individuals come together to proceed on one path. They share the same goal in life and they want to help each other attain that goal.

If you come together to be partners in living a dedicated life, a life of service, then the marriage will be made in heaven.

The true relationship of husband and wife is for each to give himself or herself completely for the sake of the other.

Once married, the couple sacrifices their I, me, and mine. She lives for his sake. He lives for her sake.

A married couple should be like two wings of one bird.

A husband and wife should not be attached to each other. They are fellow pilgrims on the spiritual path.

If God brought you a partner that does not believe what you do, adapt, adjust, accommodate, live with that person. Don't try to change that person.

Giving love to get love in return is business. Real love is a one-way street — just give with no thought of anything in return.

You can't just have sweet all of the time. Sometimes you need a little pickle.

Realize that you don't have a relationship to be happy. You are already married to your peace and joy. Let us not disturb it or divorce it to get someone else.

The Body and Health

The human body is a temple. Keep it strong and supple.

To purify the body, practice the disciplines of Hatha Yoga and take care of your diet.

God has given you the body as a ladder to climb up. The ladder itself is not going upstairs. But you need to go up, so you have to take care of it.

Health is your birthright, not disease.

The main reason to fall sick is stress. A stressful mind is full of "I want this, I want that," unkind thoughts, selfish thoughts.

A really healthy person takes everything in life as a game.

Do not be confined to your body. The body is a sort of prison that limits your Self. The mind can rise above it.

The body is just a reflection of the thought-waves of the mind.

Good thoughts make good bodies. Bad thoughts make bad bodies.

Think good thoughts. Then your actions will be clean, then your body will be clean.

To control the mind, go through the body.

Drink eight 8-oz glasses of water a day.

Many ailments today are caused by not drinking enough water.

Juicer? Chew, sir.

Chew your liquids and liquefy your solids. Then your food is mixed well with saliva and digested better.

Once the mind is controlled, you can do whatever you want with the body.

The mind can cure any part of the body.

Pranayama – Breathing Techniques

By regular practice of *pranayama,* we are able to not only control and direct the *prana* (vital force) that functions within us, but the universal *prana* as well.

Prana is the vital force that makes up the entire cosmos. It is the *Parashakti* or Cosmic Power.

Pure *prana* is everywhere but you must take it in with something, such as food, air, or ether *(akasha).*

The amount of *prana* is the same in pure air as in impure air.

When you breathe in, the *prana* comes in with the air. Nothing can pollute the *prana* but you can pollute the air.

If you can regulate your *prana* and raise it to the crown of the head, the body will glow.

When your *nadis* (subtle nerves) are purified well through *pranayama*, you will feel a natural joy in life and you will not fall sick.

Pain and Suffering

No pain, no gain.

Without destruction there is no construction.

If pain is there, you are not going to reduce an ounce of pain by your fear.

If you are afraid, the pain brings a big cost.

If you are undergoing pain, say to yourself, "So I made a mistake, now I am purging it out. Without pain, I cannot get rid of the problem."

If you cannot accept pain, ask God to help you.

Problems come to you to test you.

The minute you decide to follow a spiritual life, all the tests come.

God will never give any test that you cannot pass.

Nature never created a problem without a solution.

When your attachments or aversions cause problems, you remember God.

When things don't turn out the way you hoped, at least remember that is because some Higher Force wanted it to be different.

If the body does not get healed, that's the way God wants it. Accept it.

It's a universal Law: Whatever you deserve, you will get and whatever you do not deserve, you will not get.

Mistakes are good. They make you grow. Just don't make the same mistakes again and again.

Make a mistake. Learn the lesson from it. Find out what you need to know.

Each mistake, each failure, is a stepping stone to success.

Only by mistakes do we learn – like children falling down before they learn to walk.

Making mistakes is good but admitting them is a great quality.

All wrongs lead to one right: "I don't want to be selfish."

Do not hesitate to receive the suffering. When will you give up? When the pain gets too bad.

Until you get burned, you will go near the fire.

Life is like a mother washing a little child. If you struggle and try to avoid getting cleaned, soap will get into your eyes and the mother will just hold you tighter and continue to scrub.

Forgetting that there will be pain behind pleasure is the problem.

Pleasure comes with pain as a tail. Pain comes with pleasure as a tail. They are two sides of the same coin.

Know that the world is a mixture of pleasure and pain. Once you know that, then you can play the game.

The person who doesn't look for pleasure and who knows it is natural to get pain, will never be pained.

You get pained because you are not expecting it. The same is true for pleasure.

Pain is impermanent. Pleasure is impermanent. Everything changes. Nothing is permanent. Like a river, everything is flowing. If you are in the river, you get swept away.

Rising above this worldly pleasure and pain means on that upper level there is an eternal joy.

If you can't return goodness to the person that hurts you, what kind of civilized person are you?

If you want to file a legal suit, sue God. God is the culprit who is working behind the person that offended you.

When someone hurts you, it is a test for you. God is testing you through that person. There is no reason to blame the other person. Blame God.

If you want to be a good Yogi, a lover of God, return all the love you can to those who hurt you. That will teach them a lesson.

The best way to punish someone who has hurt you is to return goodness for hurt.

Make someone who has hurt you ashamed of his deed by returning good to him.

Karma - Action and Reaction

Your destiny is the sum total of past karma. Accept it and purge it out.

You do not need to know your destiny. But you need to know where you want to go.

When we finish our karma in one body, we move into another body.

To create new karma or to rise beyond all karma, you have to come back here as a human being, get caught up again in the three *gunas* (qualities of nature), and learn all the lessons.

Tracing the path of karma is like tracing the footprints of the birds in the sky.

God is not there to punish you. Karma comes only to make you learn by your mistakes.

Jnana Yoga – The Yoga of Wisdom

Whatever comes, just be a witness to it.

Be a constant witness of your own life. By witnessing, you will not be affected by your thoughts.

To maintain your peace and joy, you need to have spiritual vision where you see God behind everything, and worldly vision where you see the transitory forms and situations.

You can maintain your peace and joy always if you have the double vision of an actor in a play: you know who you are essentially and you play a role which is non-essential to who you really are.

Hanuman said, "Whenever I think I am the body, then let me be Your servant. Whenever I think that I am the Soul, let me be a part of You. When I think I am the Self, then I am You. Give me the knowledge to remember this because I dwell in these three levels.

Behind the changes that are constantly changing is the never changing One. That is the Truth that you are searching for.

To realize everything is the Self, you must have realized the Self within.

If you cannot see God within, you cannot see God without.

God is the only reality. All the rest is a dream.

When shall I see Thee? When "I" ceases to be.

Separate your identification from the body and mind. That separation is liberation. You liberate yourself from the mind's clutches and you remember your true nature.

Ignorance or not knowing is the cause of all the problems.

Ego is ignorance.

Freedom or bondage comes as you think.

Thinking is the beginning but it is not enough. Experiencing is necessary.

You can't attain freedom from action by conscious thinking or by applying your ego. Only by your total detachment from thinking and ego is that freedom known.

A *Jivanmukta* (God-realized person) is liberated from the bondage of his or her own mind and senses.

The Truth cannot be spoken, and whatever is spoken is not the Truth.

The Supreme *Brahman* (the Absolute) can never be expressed or expounded, it can only be realized.

The best way to talk about Truth is keeping quiet.

We say we cannot talk about God, but still we must somehow satisfy our minds. Thus we slowly widen our limited understanding more and more until one day it becomes unlimited.

Once you realize the universal Truth, you embrace the entire world as your family.

Once you really understand the absolute Truth and submit yourself to that Truth, then there is nothing for you to attain or fulfill in this world; all your so-called duties are over.

The spiritual renunciate's main interest is knowing the Essence.

Knowledge of the Essence is sacred knowledge. Secular knowledge without sacred knowledge always creates problems.

Humility is the greatest virtue of a wise person.

The receiving hand is always lower than the giving hand.

Light

The light is a formless form. The entire universe grows and survives with the light and that light shines within also.

Stand with your back to the light. You will see your shadow. Try to catch your shadow it will run away from you. Turn around and go toward the light; gently look over your shoulder, you will see your shadow running after you. Seek the Light first and then everything will be running after you.

It is the darkness that makes us look for light.

We are all saints, but some express it and others do not. Like a light behind a glass chimney, if the chimney is colored, you see colored light. If the chimney is dirty, you cannot see the light.

See the same Light, the same Spirit dwelling everywhere in everything or, to be more accurate, as everything.

God is the Light of awareness, the Light of our Consciousness, the One who enlightens everything and everybody.

Enlightenment is just making yourself light.

Religion

Religion means "return to your source." What is your source? God. Who is God? Your own Spirit, your own personal Self.

Religion means returning to your Source. The vehicle doesn't matter.

Spiritual life means we are all made of the same Spirit.

The purpose of religion is to educate us about our spiritual unity.

No two individuals have the same religion. Each mind is different and you create your religion with your mind.

The practitioners of different religions need to go deep into their own religion before they can understand the oneness in all.

If you know the purpose of your own religion, then you will know that other people have the same purpose.

Fundamental Truth is the same in all religions.

Truth is one, paths are many. Stick to one path, but do not say to others that this is the only one. Recognize all other paths and respect them.

The essence of Yoga and all the faiths and traditions is to be easeful in body, peaceful in mind, and useful in life.

Life and Death

Live the present. Enjoy the golden present. The past is vomit. You don't need to eat it again. The future is far away.

He who worries about the harvest fails to sow the seed now. Sow the seed now and the future will take care of itself.

Worrying about the future means you are missing the present.

A quality of a *Jivanmukta* (God-realized person) is to never worry about the future.

People do not know how to live a single minute, but their thoughts are millions and millions.

When you live for yourself, you're not really living.

What are you afraid of? Death? You should be afraid of not living!

The body is a vehicle, an RV—recreational vehicle. You use it until it breaks down and then you leave it and go somewhere else.

Fear of death comes when you are attached to your old car.

No one ever dies. Only the body dies. It is a composed object that decomposes.

At the death of the body, the soul flies away from the body as a bird from its shell.

You have to die to live.

Guru

When the student is ready, the Guru will come.

If you come to the Guru with nothing, you go with everything. If you come with something, you go with just that something.

If you bring your head to the head of the Guru, there is repulsion. If you bring your head to his feet, there is attraction (as with the poles of a magnet).

The great liberators of the world – Krishna, Rama, Shankara, Jesus, Moses, Buddha – do not liberate us. They give us the idea, we accept it, apply it to our lives, and free ourselves.

The teacher is not the Guru. The teaching is the Guru.

If you do not have faith in a practice, at least have faith in the one who gave you the practice. Then there is no room for doubt.

You cannot think of the Guru without him hearing you.

The Guru is always there to guide you, to tell you what to do and what not to do, but your egoistic mind blocks it.

You all have the Guru inside you. He always guides you, talks to you. Unfortunately, you don't take time to listen to that. Somebody else also talks to you. If you can calm down that somebody else, then you will be able to listen to the Guru within.

If you have the eyes to see me, I'm here and everywhere.

Epilogue

by Rev. Prem Anjali, Ph.D.

Those who have been blessed to call themselves disciples and devotees of His Holiness Sri Swami Satchidanandaji know the special Grace of having a Satguru. Not only a Satguru, Sri Gurudev is what is referred to as a *Trikala Jnani*—a sage who has the knowledge of past, present and future.

Sri Gurudev gave many signs over the past years, and particularly over the past six months, of His impending *Mahasamadhi*. In February 2002, Sri Gurudev gave His grandson, Mr. A. Murugesan (Murugesh) all the necessary instructions for the *Mahasamadhi* rituals. It took from February until the beginning of August to gather all the required items in India. Four days prior to His *Mahasamadhi,* Sri Gurudev was informed that all the supplies were carefully gathered and ready in Chennai (Madras). Murugesh asked Sri Gurudev if the items should be shipped by sea or, since He was en route to Chennai, if He wished to check them prior to shipping. Sri Gurudev's reply was: "Let them be kept ready in Chennai, and I will bring them back with me to Yogaville." These materials accompanied Sri Gurudev's body on the return to Yogaville for the *Mahasamadhi* ceremonies.

Sri Gurudev knew it, He planned it, and prepared His disciples brilliantly for His *Mahasamadhi.*

I have had the incredible grace and blessing to serve Sri Gurudev as His personal assistant and the executive director of His international secretariat for the past 24 years. In addition to serving Sri Gurudev in the Ashrams, I traveled extensively with Him, serving Him and His global service to the best of my ability. During these many years, I had the opportunity to hear Sri Gurudev speak about numerous subjects, including that of leaving His body. I poured over my notes on this subject—Sri Gurudev's recent comments, notes of conversations I made between Sri Gurudev and particular devotees, as well as transcripts of talks where He spoke about this occurrence.

Over many years, Sri Gurudev spoke extensively about the Guru-disciple relationship. He often addressed the theme in a particular way, explaining that: "The Guru is not the body, not even the mind. The real Guru is the teaching. That Guru will always be with you. He will never die. He will never disappear from your life."

The teaching that "The real Guru is the teaching" forms the basis of His philosophy on the subject of the Guru-disciple relationship, but it does not necessarily address the more devotional aspect of Sri Gurudev's direct and very active relationship with His devotees. In a moment, we will consider this very subtle and yet most important distinction in understanding Sri Gurudev's clear, eternal promises to those devoted to Him as their Satguru.

Many people have asked me questions since Sri Gurudev's *Mahasamadhi,* such as: "Who is replacing Sri Gurudev?" "Did Sri Gurudev name a successor?" "Who is in charge now?" "Will Sri Gurudev reincarnate to be with us again?"

Sri Gurudev answered all these questions recently, and over the years, in discussions that I will share with you.

First, there is the nearly fathomless relationship between a Guru and His devotees, according to Sri Gurudev. During the summer of 2002, Sri Gurudev spent a lot of time meeting with devotees who came to Yogaville from far and wide to have His *Darshan.* He gave each of them a consistent message. I recall particularly two devotees, Suguna Feldman and her daughter Padma, who came from Santa Fe, New

Mexico, in early July to visit Sri Gurudev. They were taking leave of Sri Gurudev, and I told them I'd go outside and pull the car up to take them back to the Lotus Guest House. I pulled the car up, but they had not come out yet–although, a minute before, they were right behind me. They emerged in a few minutes, got into the car, and said, "Wow, that was something!" I asked what they meant. Suguna replied, "As we were leaving, Gurudev called us back in. He took out some *vibhuti* (holy ash) and applied it to our foreheads. Then, He placed one hand on my shoulder and the other hand on Padma's shoulder. He looked deeply into our eyes and said, 'Remember, I will be with you always.'"

This is the same message Sri Gurudev gave to many devotees over the months prior to His *Mahasamadhi*. It was not unlike Sri Gurudev to say this, particularly when invited to attend a function or occasion in which He was not able to participate physically. He often asked me to let those inviting Him know that He would be with them "in Spirit" for this or that occasion. And I had no doubt that Sri Gurudev meant that literally. Even more, in these recent months, this was an utterance that took on deeper meaning.

On 10 August, Amma Rasiah who is in charge of Sri Gurudev's Fine Arts Society, phoned Him in India to seek His blessings for the annual *Bharata Natyam* dance camp's graduation program. This is a program that Sri Gurudev often attended; but, due to His travels this year, He was in India at the time of the graduation. Amma said to Sri Gurudev, "We are seeking Your blessings as usual for the graduation this evening."

Sri Gurudev replied, "Yes, Amma, you have all my blessings and I will be there with you in Spirit." Then, Amma, not wanting to take more of Gurudev's time since He was busy with His travel program, thanked Him and was about to hang up the phone. Suddenly, and uncustomarily, Sri Gurudev called out to Amma and said, "Amma, one more thing. Remember: I will **always** be with you all in Spirit."

Over the years, Sri Gurudev often spoke to me and to others about the limitation of His physical body. He said, "In a way, all the great sages, saints, and prophets function better when they leave this limited body, which is almost a prison."

In the early 1970s, Sri Gurudev was already mentioning how much more service He would do without the constraints of the body. Amma Kidd, who served as Sri Gurudev's secretary during that time told me the following story.

Amma accompanied Sri Gurudev to the hospital to visit Mataji (Swami Gurucharananandaji) who was recuperating from an illness. On her nightstand, Mataji had placed pictures of Sri Gurudev and other saints. Sri Gurudev looked at them all with great interest. Pointing at a picture of Saint Thérèse de Lisieux, He inquired who she was. Mataji explained, and Amma told Gurudev that Saint Thérèse was practically hidden from the world during her life on earth, her saintliness known by only a very few. It was only after her passing that her "public life" began with the sudden flourishing of innumerable apparitions, miracles, and the worldwide publishing of her book.

Sri Gurudev became very silent and finally said: "It is true; the body is a limitation. The time will come when I will no longer be confined in the body. Then you people will see what great things will happen. Great things."

On a more recent occasion, just a few days prior to Sri Gurudev's departure to India in July, Amma Kidd sent Him a letter by fax. She often proceeded this way when just informing Him of things that needed no reply. That evening, she was surprised to find a message from Sri Gurudev on her voicemail, saying: "Hello Amma, this is me. I received your fax." The silence that followed was broken with the emphatic, thunderous utterance: "Remember you will never be without me. Never! The body may go, but I am always with you. Always!" Upon hearing the message, Amma felt a grip in her heart, but quickly attributed the message to the fact that He was going on a trip.

One of my primary duties over the years was to look after the health of Sri Gurudev's body. While He had a tremendous respect for the body as a temple, He had no patience for too much emphasis upon it. Sri Gurudev's body enjoyed good health and tremendous vigor for service; and everyone knows what an active, vital and energetic life He lived. Sri Gurudev was always on the go. From the moment He left India in the 1950s, He was continually traveling through Southeast Asia on speaking tours. He was moving, moving, moving. I used to tease Him saying He came into this world with wheels on His heels.

His service enlivened Him. It was His lifebreath. Vitally serving, He circled the globe many times. Sri Gurudev never went anywhere uninvited; He constantly received invitations from many, many organizations worldwide. He was always on the go—speaking at Yoga conferences, peace summits, interfaith gatherings and so on. It was a service that He loved and was uniquely destined to perform.

After *Guru Poornima* in July 2002, Sri Gurudev set off for a tour of five countries, including India. He was hospitalized suddenly in India. The evening before Sri Gurudev attained *Mahasamadhi,* He explained to those gathered around Him, "I can serve better without this body. I will be free to serve millions without the restrictions of this physical body, which is tying me down now. It will be a great blessing if my soul can depart from the body here on the soil of Mother India and then go back to America."

Sri Gurudev's Spirit pervades and His Presence is clearly felt by many, many devotees. He is fulfilling every promise He made. He is forever our Satguru, the Spiritual Head and Guide of Satchidananda Ashram-Yogaville and the entire Integral Yoga organization. He made it very clear that He was only "dropping the body" in order to serve us more fully and completely and unimpeded. He named no spiritual successor because there was no need to as He is actively with us.

Regarding the administration and management of the Ashram and organization, that continues as it has for years. More than ten years ago, Sri Gurudev delegated the responsibilities of the administration and daily operations to a capable team of devoted disciples. For five years, this team has been ably led by the Ashram

President, Swami Asokanandaji. Sri Gurudev continues to guide the spiritual development of all His devotees and this organization.

As to the question about whether Sri Gurudev will "incarnate" again to guide His devotees, He made it very clear to many of us that the reason He was "dropping the body" was to be able to serve more fully and widely. He never said He would reincarnate here and now. In fact, He stated: "When I leave my body, I will continue to guide you from a higher level."

That does not mean that when we, as devotees, leave our bodies, we will never be united with our beloved Guru again. Sri Gurudev inhabited a particular form in which we could have His *Darshan* in this birth. In our future births, we may encounter Him in different forms.

In fact, Sri Gurudev addressed this very point when He said: "In every incarnation the same Guru may appear in a different form. That's why many a time when you meet your Master, or when He or She meets you, you feel that you have known the Guru for ages. You don't see a new, unknown person. Simply stated, your memories are not vivid because of the change of the body. But if the mind is very clear, you can have vivid memories of that. The Guru-disciple relationship never ends. It's always there. Whether the Guru leaves the body, or the disciple dies. That relationship is eternal and Guru and disciple can never be separated."

May each and every one of us be blessed with a more profound understanding of this eternal Guru-disciple relationship. May this immortal bond bring us into deeper communion with Sri Gurudev's ever-present Spirit. May Sri Gurudev's Love, Blessings, and Teachings ever fill our hearts and guide our lives. And may we continue to express our gratitude and devotion to Him through our service to the entire creation.

Om Shanthi.

Jai Sri Sat Guru Satchidanandaji Maharaj Ki!

"You Will Never Be Without Me:"

by His Holiness Sri Swami Satchidananda

"When I leave my body I will continue to guide you from a higher level. When you are in the Guru's physical presence you think that the guidance is coming from the physical side. No, spiritual help need not depend on the physical body. If that is so, then Jesus and Buddha will not be helping anybody anymore. On the other hand, it is mostly after their physical death they seem to be doing a lot of work. When the body is not there then you begin to understand something beyond that body. Most of the teachers became well-known and were able to help most of the disciples after their physical death.

"Physical death is not the culmination of the journey. Lord Jesus in His own life demonstrates that. It's the body that got crucified but nobody can touch the astral or spiritual body.

"The spiritual body is still in the physical body. It's almost like I'm wearing a robe. Your perception stops at the robe and you couldn't go beyond that. But when I take this robe out, then you are able to see something more inside; something more real. Once the physical body is gone, then those who have the capacity to see, will see the spiritual body. It is the spiritual body that is able to go anywhere and everywhere, moving freely.

"When we are out of this body we realize how happy we are. We realize the whole universe is ours. You can go wherever you want. Here in the body, if I want to go from one place to another place, I need a car, a plane, this and that. I can't even travel easily. If I want to pick up something, I am limited by what is within the reach of my body, that's all. My hand cannot reach farther. But when I am out of this body I can reach anywhere and everywhere. Space and time mean nothing in that level.

"The *Bhagavad Gita* clearly states, 'The Self cannot be wetted by water, burnt by fire, cut by a sword.' When the body is dead, the spirit is not dead. So here we see the immortal principle, the immortality of the soul.

"The *Thirukkural* says, 'Death is like a bird breaking the shell and it comes out and flies away.' A bird will not be happy if it is confined in that little eggshell. One day it has to pry it open, break it and fly out. So, a soul wants to soar but the body is a fetter.

"Another example given in the *Thirukkural* is that the bird was in the cage and people only saw the cage. But when the cage got broken the bird flew away. You may say the bird got resurrected. It was completely covered by the cage. You were not able to see the bird inside. Once the cage got broken you are able to see the bird flying away.

"Evolved souls, enlightened beings like Jesus and other great sages and saints, when they depart from the body they can easily reach everybody. They can do more great things than they did while they were in the body.

"The time will come when I will no longer be confined in the body and can easily reach everybody. Then you people will see what great things will happen.

"You should be able to receive the Guru's Guidance from a higher level. When would you be able to do that? When you have that communication. You communicate with His astral and spiritual body, with His thoughts, with His Teachings. You may not see me but you know what I would be telling you in a given circumstance, is it not so?

"The Guru-disciple relationship never ends. It's always there. Whether the Guru leaves the body, or the disciple dies. That relationship is eternal and Guru and disciple can never be separated.

"In every incarnation the same Guru may appear in a different form. That's why many a time when you meet your Master, or when He meets you, you feel that you have known Him for ages. You don't see Him as a new, unknown person. But these memories are not vivid because of the change of the body. But if the mind is very clear you can have vivid memories of that.

"Remember you will never be without me, never! The body may go, but I am always with you. Always!"

His Holiness Sri Swami Satchidananda

His Holiness Sri Swami Satchidananda (Sri Gurudev) is one of the most revered Yoga Masters of our time. Sri Gurudev's teachings and spirit guide us toward a life of Peace, both individual and universal, and to religious harmony among all people. Invited to come to the US in 1966 by artist Peter Max and filmmaker Conrad Rooks, Sri Gurudev was quickly embraced by young Americans looking for lasting peace during the turbulent 1960's. In 1969, He opened the Woodstock Festival with the words: "The whole world is watching you. The entire world is going to know what the American youth can do for humanity. America is helping everybody in the material field, but the time has come for America to help the whole world with spirituality also." The peaceful atmosphere that prevailed throughout the event was often attributed to His blessings and message.

Sri Gurudev was ordained as a monk in 1949 by His master, His Holiness Sri Swami Sivananda Maharaj, founder of the Divine Life Society, Rishikesh, India. From the beginning of His spiritual service, Sri Gurudev was a leader in the interfaith movement. His motto, "Truth is One, Paths are Many," is an integral part of His teachings. For more than forty-five years, He sponsored interfaith worship services and conferences. His teachings advocate respecting and honoring all faiths. Sri Gurudev was invited to share His message of peace with such world leaders and dignitaries as former U.S. Presidents Jimmy Carter, George Bush and Bill Clinton; His Holiness Pope Paul VI, His Holiness Pope John Paul II, His Holiness the Dalai Lama, and former Secretary-General of the United Nations U Thant.

Sri Gurudev is the Founder and Spiritual Guide for the worldwide Integral Yoga Institutes. Integral Yoga, as taught by Sri Gurudev, combines various methods of Yoga, including Hatha Yoga, selfless service, meditation, prayer, and a 5,000-year-old philosophy that helps one find the peace and joy within. Integral Yoga is the foundation for Dr. Dean Ornish's landmark work in reversing heart disease and Dr. Michael Lerner's noted Commonweal Cancer Help program.

In 1979, Sri Gurudev was inspired to create a permanent place where all people could come to realize their essential oneness. He established Satchidananda Ashram—Yogaville near Charlottesville, Virginia. The community is founded on His teachings, which include the principles of non-violence and universal harmony.

The focal point of Yogaville is the Light Of Truth Universal Shrine (LOTUS), which was dedicated in 1986. This unique interfaith Shrine honors the Spirit that unites all the world religions, while celebrating their diversity. People from all faiths and backgrounds, from all over the world, come there to meditate and pray.

Sri Gurudev served on the advisory boards of the Temple of Understanding, the Interfaith Center of New York, the Center for International Dialogue, and numerous other world peace and interfaith organizations. Over the years, He received many honors for His public service, including the Albert Schweitzer Humanitarian Award and the Anti-Defamation League Humanitarian Award. In October 1994, on the occasion of the 125th birth anniversary of Mahatma Gandhi, He was awarded the highest citation of the Bharatiya Vidya Bhavan. He was named an Honorary Patron, joining the list of such luminaries to receive this award as Dr. S. Radhakrishnan, Mother Teresa, and His Holiness the Dalai Lama. Also, in 1994, He was named "Hindu of the Year" by *Hinduism Today* magazine. In 1996, He was presented with the Juliet Hollister Interfaith Award at the United Nations. In April 2002, He was honored with the prestigious U Thant Peace Award. Previous recipients of this award include Pope John Paul II,

Mother Teresa, Archbishop Desmond Tutu, and Nelson Mandela. He is the author of many books, including *Integral Yoga Hatha, To Know Your Self, The Living Gita,* and *The Golden Present* and is the subject of two biographies, *Apostle of Peace* and *Portrait of a Modern Sage.*

Born in South India in 1914, Sri Gurudev attained *Mahasamadhi* in 2002.